E
RAU
Reader

Climbing

by **Dana Meachen Rau**

Reading Consultant: Nanci R. Vargus, Ed. D.

Marshall Cavendish
Benchmark
New York

Picture Words

arms

banana

firemen

ladder

legs

monkey

mountains

nest

playground

railing

roof

slide

squirrel

stairs

tree

You use your 🖐️🖐️ and 🦵🦵
to climb.

Climbing takes you up.

A worker climbs up a .

He fixes the .

 climb up a /.

They help put a fire out.

People climb up .

They see a lot from the top.

People climb up .

They hold on to the .

A  can climb a .

It eats a  at the top.

A  can climb a ,
too.

It makes a in the branches.

Kids climb at the .

They take turns on the net.

You can climb, too.

Now slide down the .

Words to Know

climb (klime)
to use your arms and legs
to go up

top the highest part of something

worker (WUR-kur)
someone who fixes things

Find Out More

Books

Brown, Marc. *Buster Climbs the Walls*. Boston: Little Brown and Company, 2005.

Gorman, Jaqueline Laks. *The Playground*. Milwaukee: Weekly Reader Early Learning Library, 2005.

McDaniel, Melissa. *Monkeys*. Tarrytown, NY: Benchmark Books, 2004.

Munsch, Robert N. *Up, Up, Down!* New York: Scholastic, 2002.

Videos

Neale, Ann. *Amazing Monkeys and Apes*. DK Vision.

Web Sites

Playground Safety
http://kidshealth.org/parent/firstaid_safe/outdoor/playground.html

Rock Climbing Schools for Kids
http://gorp.away.com/gorp/publishers/ftf/cli_kids.htm

Squirrel Place
http://www.squirrels.org/

About the Author

Dana Meachen Rau is an author, editor, and illustrator. A graduate of Trinity College in Hartford, Connecticut, she has written more than one hundred books for children, including nonfiction, biographies, early readers, and historical fiction. She likes to go rock climbing near her home in Burlington, Connecticut.

About the Reading Consultant

Nanci R. Vargus, Ed.D, wants all children to enjoy reading. She used to teach first grade. Now she works at the University of Indianapolis. Nanci helps young people become teachers. Nanci enjoys gentle climbs in our national parks, but her daughter Abigail met the big challenge of Mount Kilaminjaro.

Marshall Cavendish Benchmark
99 White Plains Road
Tarrytown, NY 10591-9001
www.marshallcavendish.us

All Internet sites were correct at the time of printing.

Library of Congress Cataloging-in-Publication Data

Rau, Dana Meachen, 1971–
Climbing / by Dana Meachen Rau.
     p. cm. — (Benchmark rebus)
Summary: "Easy to read text with rebuses explores things that climb"—Provided by publisher.
Includes bibliographical references.
ISBN-13: 978-0-7614-2318-8
ISBN-10: 0-7614-2318-4
1. Vocabulary—Juvenile literature. I. Title. II. Series.
PE1449.R339 2006
428.1—dc22
        2005031270

Editor: Christine Florie
Editorial Director: Michelle Bisson
Art Director: Anahid Hamparian
Series Designer: Virginia Pope

Photo research by Connie Gardner

Rebus images provided courtesy of *Dorling Kindersley.*

Cover photo Royalty Free/CORBIS

The photographs in this book are used with permission and through the courtesy of:
Corbis: p. 5 Dan Mason; p. 9 Ralf-Finn Hestoft; p. 11 John Henley; p. 13 James P. Blair; p. 17 Gary W. Carter; p. 19 Jennie Woodcock/Reflections PhotoLibrary; p. 21 Ariel Skelley; *Getty:* p. 7 Brand X Pictures; *Peter Arnold:* p. 15 Mason Fischer.

Printed in Malaysia
1 3 5 6 4 2